# The Catholic Guide To Confession

Archbishop Daniel E. Pilarczyk

Our Sunday Visitor Publishing Division
Our Sunday Visitor, Inc.
Huntington, Indiana 46750

This work is adapted from a four-part series of meditations on the Sacrament of Reconciliation by Archbishop Daniel E. Pilarczyk of Cincinnati, president of the National Conference of Catholic Bishops, which appeared in *Our Sunday Visitor* magazine in December 1989.



Our Sunday Visitor Publishing Division
Our Sunday Visitor, Inc.
200 Noll Plaza
Huntington, Indiana 46750

International Standard Book Number: 0-87973-164-4

*Cover design by Rebecca J. O'Brien*

PRINTED IN THE UNITED STATES OF AMERICA

164

## CONTENTS

*ONE*

# Celebrating Our Rescue From Sin

IN THE DAYS of sailing ships, one of the worst things that could happen to a seafarer was to be marooned. If a sailor became too troublesome to the captain — or if a captain became too troublesome to the sailors — he would be set ashore alone, on a desolate island or coast, and left to his fate. Perhaps enough food and water for a week or so would be left with the victim, but basically he was on his own. Occasionally the person marooned would be rescued, but most of the time he would die of hunger, thirst, and exposure, in many cases having gone insane in the process.

The reason why being marooned was such a terrible fate is, of course, that human beings were not meant to live alone. No one except the most resourceful person can long provide for his own physical needs if he is all alone. But, in addition to that, there is the psychological need for human company. Even the most antisocial person needs other people around. We simply cannot supply for ourselves that which we need if there is no one to share the burden with us and cooperate with us. For all practical purposes, being marooned was the same as a death sentence.

To some degree, each one of us has been marooned at some time in our lives. It is not that somebody casts us ashore on a desert island, but rather that we put ourselves into a situation of being more or less cut off from the resources and the relationships we need in order to enjoy a full and true human existence.

**Sin: Not So Much a Matter of Breaking Rules as of Breaking Relationships**

When we have a tiff with someone we love — friend, relative, spouse — we find ourselves cut off from that person, perhaps only for a few minutes, perhaps for longer. But during the time that our relationship is damaged, we somehow find ourselves alone to a greater or lesser extent. We have marooned ourselves. We are separated from the person with whom we have quarreled.

There are other ways to maroon ourselves. The thief, for example, cuts himself off from human society to the extent that he becomes a law unto himself, taking what is not really his and needing to be alone so that he can keep what he has taken. The woman who thinks that she is better than everybody else is cut off from those whom she despises as surely as if she were on a desert island. The violent person — whether the violence be physical or psychological — enters a sphere of psychological isolation that others are not allowed to penetrate.

We can even maroon ourselves from God. A life in which God has no part, and in which, consequently, our calling to be agents of God's love is disregarded is really a life alone, a life in which there is no purpose, a life which is condemned to try to provide for itself that which can only come from outside and beyond it.

This experience of radical loneliness is well-known to modern psychology, which speaks of it not as being marooned but as alienation, of becoming an outsider, of making oneself foreign. Christian religious tradition speaks of the same reality when it speaks of sin.

Sin is not so much a matter of breaking rules as it is a matter of breaking relationships. Every sin we can name has to do with being related: related to the world, related to other human beings, related to ourselves, related to God. To what ever extent we sin, we are cutting ourselves off from something or someone, we are casting ourselves into isolation from what we were meant to be. Sin is ultimately a rejection of relationship, a rejection of love, a refusal to love God in response to the love God gives us, a refusal to love others as God loves us, a refusal to love the world as God loves it. Sin consists in deliberately putting ourselves outside.

**Reconciliation: Bringing Us Out of Alienation, Isolation, Loneliness**

What the marooned sailor wants more than anything else is to be rescued, to be freed from his isolation, to get back together again with the human companionship that he needs. The sinner needs to be rescued, too. He or she needs to have injured relationships healed, to be brought back from alienation and loneliness. The sinner needs reconciliation.

The root meaning of the word "reconciliation" is "calling together again." In the context of our human sinfulness, reconciliation has to do with bringing us back, with putting us in touch again with what we were meant to be, with bringing us out of isolation — partial or complete — and setting us into a healed relationship with ourselves, with our world, with our brothers and sisters, and with the Lord.

There are many ways and many degrees of being called together again, of being rescued from the loneliness of sin, but among the most clear and explicit of all is that special encounter with the Lord which the Church offers us in the Sacrament of Reconciliation.

In order to appreciate what happens in the Sacrament of Reconciliation, there are a few things we need to be clear about.

**First, All of Us Are Sinners, and Second, No Sin Is Strictly Private**

The first is that we are all sinners. We may not be murderers, thieves or blasphemers, but, to a greater or lesser extent, we all abuse the gifts God has given us. We have an inborn inclination to zero in on ourselves in a destructive way, to isolate ourselves in selfishness, and we have all given in to that inclination. Sometimes we sin in what we do: in the sharp word, the covetous action, the way we manipulate other people. Sometimes we sin in what we do not do: in our neglect of God in prayer or in our unwillingness to use the opportunities, which are presented to us, to serve others. Sometimes we sin in our fundamental personal attitudes and habits: in the laziness that we do nothing to correct, in taking our gifts for granted, in putting ourselves so consistently first. None of us is everything that we could be if we stood rightly in the relationships that God has given us.

It is not comforting to think about our sinfulness, but if we don't, we run the risk of finding ourselves spiritually marooned without even knowing how we got there.

Second, no sin is strictly private. Everything we do has some effect on our relationships. The choices and decisions we make — or do not make — have their effect on our relationship with God, on our attitudes toward the world, on our rapport with other people. As members of the community of believers that is the Church, we are called to be holy as Christ is holy and to love others as He loved them. To the extent that we are unfaithful to this calling, we weaken the whole community. No sin is my own affair alone. No sin is just between my neighbor and me. No sin is just between God and me.

**A Gift From God, and Therefore a Real Reason for Celebration**

For this reason, reconciliation is not something that we can do for ourselves. Because every sin ultimately involves relationships with creation, Church, brothers and sisters, the Lord, and, of course, with my own destiny in the Lord, the healing of sin necessarily involves all of these relationships as well. Sin is something we do for ourselves. Reconciliation is not. It comes to us as a gift, ultimately as a gift from God.

Finally, because this rescue from the isolation of sin is a gift, it is something to celebrate. One of the most crucial aspects of the Good News that Jesus came to share with us is that God loves us so much that He is willing to forgive us any sin, that God is willing to take us back no matter how far we have wandered, that God is so interested in us that there is nothing we can do to make Him write us off. In Jesus' parables of the lost sheep, the lost coin, and the lost (or prodigal) son, the one lesson is that God is happy to get us back when we have gone astray. God celebrates the reconciliation of the sinner and invites us to celebrate it as well.

All these elements — our sinfulness, it simplications in all our relationships, the generous initiative of the Lord in freeing us from the isolation of sin, and, above all, the joy of the Lord in the return of the sinner — are part of the Sacrament of Reconciliation.

Many Catholics look on going to confession as a burden, as something one has to do once in a while. Such a view focuses on only a part of what is involved in the sacrament. The real kernel of the sacrament is not our sinfulness, but the love, the forgiveness and the joy that God offers us in it.

When a marooned sailor is brought back from what could have been terminal isolation, he doesn't concentrate on his former plight. He celebrates his rescue. In the same way, we are called to *celebrate* the Sacrament of Reconciliation.

*TWO*

## Meeting Our God in the Confessional

CELEBRATION generally involves a lot of people. True, a husband and wife may choose to celebrate a wedding anniversary by themselves, but more often when we speak of "celebrating" something, we understand that more than one or two persons are going to be included. In fact, the root meaning of the word implies crowds or throngs of people.

It will be easier for us to understand the Sacrament of Reconciliation if we are clear about who participates in it and how. After that we will see more clearly what exactly happens when the sacrament is celebrated.

The main participant in the celebration of the Sacrament of Reconciliation is the Lord God. This is easy enough to understand if we recall that our sinfulness is ultimately directed at the Lord. Everyone and everything that are affected by sin belong to God. All the relationships that we wound in our flight toward isolation are relationships that God has established for our well-being. We ourselves belong to God, and in withdrawing from what God means to us to be we are offending against God's loving purposes in our regard.

For this reason, it is God who must bring about reconciliation. Repairing relationships must always involve everyone who is part of the relationship, and the relationships that we reject or weaken by our sinfulness all involve God. Consequently, God is the main agent of reconciliation. Without God's involvement, any attempt on our part alone to retreat from alienation is meaningless.

The Sacrament of Reconciliation also involves the Church. Apart from our relationship with God, our relationship with the Church is the one that is most damaged by our sinfulness. The Church is not some sort of club offering us privileges and benefits that we may take advantage of to the extent that we choose. Rather, the Church is a living organism, a community of believers, with Jesus as its head, constituting the continuation and extension of the life of Christ. Isolating ourselves by sin damages the unity and the vigor of that organism. Instead of building up the body of Christ, our sinfulness tears it down.

**The Priest Greets the Sinner, Representing Both the Lord God and the Church Community**

All believers are harmed when one believer sins. Conversely, all believers benefit when one believer returns from wandering afar. This is why the process of reconciliation is a sacrament of the Church, because the Church is so closely involved with what sin and reconciliation are all about. This is why the Church celebrates whenever reconciliation takes place.

The representative of both the Lord God and of the Church in the Sacrament of Reconciliation is the priest. People often wonder why they have to tell their sins to the priest in order to be forgiven. Is it not enough to ask God for pardon? It is not, because it is not God alone who has been offended by our sins. The Church, too, has been involved, even if we did not consciously direct our sins against the Church. Consequently, when it comes time for reconciliation, both God and the Church must have a part in the celebration. This part is entrusted to the priest, who is ordained to represent the Lord Christ in a special way and to be leader and spokesman for Christ's people, the Church.

The other major participant in the celebration is, obviously, the sinner. Here is one who has gone off alone, who has tried to make his or her way in life by moving in a direction other than that of God and the Church. Here is one who, to a greater or lesser extent, has "known better" than God or the Church about life and friendship and world and destiny, but who has now realized that he or she is increasingly cut off from where true fulfillment lies. Every sinner in the process of repentance echoes the words of the lost son in the Gospel: "Father, I have sinned against heaven and against you. I no longer deserve to be called yours." But, like the son in the parable, the sinner is not in the role of outcast but of welcome wanderer, of one for whom the father will throw a grand party. It is important for us to keep in mind that when we come to the Sacrament of Reconciliation, we are not coming to be punished or humiliated. We are coming to be part of a celebration, and the celebration is in honor of us. These, then, are the participants in the celebration of reconciliation: the Lord God, Christ's Church, the priest as representative of the Lord and the Church community, and the penitent sinner. It is a pretty impressive gathering.

**Celebration: Word of God, Sorrow, Pardon, Peace; Praise, Thanksgiving, Mercy at Sacrament's Heart**

Let us look now at the celebration itself.

It begins with the Word of God. If it is a communal celebration of the sacrament that is taking place, there will be one or more readings from the Bible, followed by a homily from the priest. If it is an individual celebration and if there is time, the priest will read a shorter passage from Scripture. The passages chosen for this purpose focus on God's love and God's desire to forgive those who have sinned.

At the same time, they remind us that the initiative for forgiveness comes from God. Before we even existed, God loved us. Before we ever sinned, God expressed His readiness to forgive us. It is fitting that, in this context of isolation and return, the first word should be God's Word.

Then the priest asks the penitent to confess his or her sins. We are expected to name all the serious sins that we are conscious of, together with the lesser sins that are of most concern for us. The reason why we are expected to express our sins is not so that we will be suitably humiliated, but so that both the Church (through the priest) and we ourselves will know what it is we are celebrating in reconciliation.

Moreover, in speaking out our sins — all of them — we are acknowledging who and what we are. What we deliberately keep quiet about we do not take responsibility for, and what we do not take responsibility for cannot be healed. This explains why we have to mention *all* our serious sins, all those matters that have a major effect on our relationship with God and the body of Christ that is the Church. Any serious sin isolates us from God, and if we do not present every isolating element in our life to God's forgiveness, we remain cut off from God.

This moment of confessing our sins is also an appropriate time to express a general overview of our recent life in terms of God's grace: where we have been spiritually; where we see ourselves going; where we would like to be; what our major problems are; what the hindrances are that keep us from being as close to God as we would like to be, or as God would like us to be.

The priest may comment on what we have said or ask us some questions to be sure he has understood what we have said. He is not being curious, but is trying to exercise his responsibility as guide and teacher of God's people.

The priest then assigns us a penance. The penance may consist of some prayers to say or it may be some action to perform. The purpose of the penance is to help us realize that our sins have consequences; because we have sinned, we have something to make up for. Clearly, we can never completely undo the harm that we have done by our sins to ourselves or to the world or to the Church. Only God can do that. But by accepting the penance we signify that our behavior has had bad effects, and that we acknowledge those effects as our responsibility.

Next we express our sorrow. We pray an act of contrition, either in the words of a formula or in words of our own. We do this in order to be clear about what is involved in this sacramental encounter. It is not a clinical listing of our defects that we are dealing with here in the sacrament. It is, rather, a call for forgiveness, a reaching out to our loving God who is waiting for our return so that He can express His love for us. Our prayerful expression of sorrow puts our sins into the proper context to receive God's pardon.

Then the priest gives us absolution. In the name of God and of the Church, he assures us of pardon and peace. The relationships that we had injured or broken are restored. We are brought back into full communion with God and with the Church. The isolation into which we had put ourselves is reversed through the love of God for us and through the action of God's Church. We are no longer alone. We are with God and with God's people again.

In communal penance services, a common prayer of praise and thanksgiving generally follows the private confessions. When the sacrament is being celebrated individually, the priest says, "Give thanks to the Lord for He is good," and the penitent responds, "His mercy endures forever."

Praise and thanksgiving and mercy are the heart of the Sacrament of Reconciliation. In the presence of God and the Church, we are made new again, just as we were in baptism. Our sins are forgiven, we are brought back, to whatever extent was necessary, into full association with everything and everyone that we were meant to be in touch with. Jesus assures us that the angels rejoice at the return of a sinner. So does the Church. So does the sinner. It's quite a celebration.

*THREE*

## What Has Changed About Confession

WHEN WE ARE invited to a celebration, we are able to participate best if we understand what the celebration is and why it is being observed in the way that it is.

Is it an anniversary celebration or a birthday party to which we are invited? If it is a birthday party, are we expected to bring a gift? Why are gifts appropriate for a birthday? For that matter, why do we celebrate birthdays at all?

We might be able to take part in a celebration without asking all these questions, but our understanding and our appreciation of what is going on will be fuller if we are aware of what is involved.

There are questions that can be appropriately asked about the celebration of reconciliation, too, especially since there have been some changes in the way the sacrament is celebrated since the Second Vatican Council.

So what is different about the way the sacrament is celebrated now as compared to the way it was celebrated before? The Vatican II decree on the liturgy (No. 72) called for the rite and the formulas for the Sacrament of Penance to be revised so that they give "more luminous expression to both the nature and the effect of the sacrament." It took the Church a while to respond to the council's legislation. The new form of the Sacrament of Reconciliation was not published until 1974. It was the last of the sacraments to be renewed in the light of the council's directive.

**Change in Emphasis, Atmosphere, "Tonality"; Role of Scripture, Awareness of Community**

The most fundamental change in the renewed rite of the sacrament is a change in emphasis. The sacrament is still essentially the same as it was before. It is still the sacrament that Christ gave the Church. But its "tonality" is different.

Before Vatican II, there was a heavy emphasis on guilt and judgment. People went to confession to tell their sins and to get absolution. The use of the sacrament tended to be a solitary experience: telling your sins in a dark box, listening to the voice of the priest from the other side of the grille, being sure that you got the penance right, and then hearing the Latin words from the priest as he pronounced the formula of forgiveness. Many people found it a difficult experience.

Since the renewal called for by the council, the atmosphere is different.

While we must still acknowledge our sinfulness, the emphasis has shifted from guilt and self-accusation to acceptance and reconciliation. We now look on the sacrament not as just the time when we must face up to how bad we are, but more as the occasion to experience once again the love and forgiveness of God in spite of our sinfulness. The Church wants this sacrament to be a joyful event, as the other sacraments are.

This change of atmosphere is reflected in the physical arrangements. The dark box has been replaced by a warm and welcoming room where we can sit down and talk face-to-face with the priest if we choose to. Instead of the disembodied voice behind the screen, we are now able to encounter a real human person who is there to welcome us and make us feel at ease. These arrangements are meant to suggest the friendliness and receptivity of Christ, who was always glad to see the sinner and respond to the sinner's needs.

The use of Scripture in the rite of reconciliation is part of the changed atmosphere, too. It is important for us to be reminded that what is going on here is not just an encounter between me and the priest. God's ongoing concern for us is part of it, too, a concern that God's word has expressed over and over again in His relationship with His people.

Perhaps the biggest change in atmosphere, though, has been the renewed emphasis on the community's role in the sacrament. Many people found it hard to understand why they were supposed to go to confession at all, since they saw their sins as something between themselves and God alone. The renewed rite of reconciliation stresses that every sin affects the Church at large and that every acceptance of God's forgiveness on the part of an individual member of the Church has implications for the Church at large.

One expression of the community's role in the sacrament is found in the words of absolution which the priest pronounces. "God, the Father of mercies, through the death and resurrection of His Son, has reconciled the world to himself and sent the Holy Spirit among us for the forgiveness of sins; through the ministry of the Church, may God give you pardon and peace, and I absolve you from your sins. . . ."

In these words, we are reminded of God's mercy from the beginning, of our redemption by Christ, the head of the body of the Church, and of the participation of the Church in the sacramental encounter through the ministry entrusted to it by Christ. The Church is part of the absolution because the Church was affected by the sin.

The communitarian dimension of the Sacrament of Reconciliation, though, is best expressed through the communal celebrations of the revised rite. These are occasions when the priest calls the people together to hear the word of God, to look into their hearts, and to confess their sins — individually, to be sure, but in the context of a Christian community represented by all the other people who are also gathered to celebrate. In these communal celebrations, reconciliation is seen clearly not as something just between God and me, but also between me and the whole community to which I belong.

Both forms of the sacrament — the "private" confession and the communal celebrations — have something to offer. The rite of reconciliation of individual penitents offers the opportunity for a longer and more detailed encounter with the priest. It gives us a chance to reflect with the priest at greater length about the general tenor of our life and to spend a few more minutes in dialogue with him. The communal service, on the other hand, is much more expressive of the Church dimension of our sinfulness and reconciliation. We need to take advantage of both forms at various times if we are to gain the maximum benefit from the sacrament.

## Not a Grim Duty, but a Joyous Celebration of Love and Forgiveness and New Acceptance

In this change of atmosphere, the Church is trying to teach us that the Sacrament of Reconciliation is not a grim duty that we must fulfill, but a joyous celebration, a celebration of love and forgiveness, the renewal of relationships on the part of God and of God's Church. It is a celebration of coming together again with God and with our brothers and sisters in the Lord. It is a rescue from loneliness and isolation. It is a family reunion among God's family.

Is the Church, then, downplaying sin? Not at all. The celebration of the Sacrament of Reconciliation makes no sense unless there is something and someone to be reconciled. Sin is a part of the life of each of us, and to try to run away from our sinfulness is to run away from reality.

But in this renewed approach to the Sacrament of Reconciliation, the Church wants us to be aware that our sinfulness is never the last word. God and the Church always stand ready to forgive and reconcile again. We are still expected to examine our conscience carefully. We are still expected to bring to the sacrament all our serious sins, as well as the less serious ones that we are most concerned about. But that's only the beginning. It is certainly not the main element of the sacrament. The main element is the welcome and reconciliation that God offers us in and through His Church.

It is in this context that we must understand the Church's concern that children experience the Sacrament of Reconciliation before they receive their First Communion. If the Sacrament of Reconciliation is exclusively, or almost exclusively, about sin and guilt and the need for absolution, it becomes a difficult and threatening experience that we must want to shield children from for as long as possible.

But if the sacrament is a celebration of God's love for us all and a reassurance that God wants to be with us even if we have not been as good as we should have been, then it seems appropriate that children should be prepared to participate in it as early as they reasonably can.

We need to know what is going on when we take part in a celebration. We need to know what is being celebrated and how and why. The Sacrament of Reconciliation is a celebration, a celebration of God's persistent love in the face of our own inclination to run away into selfishness and isolation. It is a good celebration to understand and to be part of.

*FOUR*

# Taking Stock With the Sacrament

EVERY SO OFTEN we are invited to a celebration, and we find ourselves wondering why. Maybe I won't know the people very well. Maybe I suspect that my presence there might be an embarrassment to the other guests. I wonder whether the invitation was a mistake and whether I really ought to go.

We are inclined to think that the best way out might simply be to invent a previous commitment and decline the invitation. When God and the Church urge us to participate in the Sacrament of Reconciliation, we may find ourselves asking similar questions: Is this meant for me? Should I go?

There are two fundamental reasons why we should participate in the celebration of the Sacrament of Reconciliation.

## The Need to Acknowledge and Examine Weaknesses and to Experience the Lord's Loving Embrace

The first is that we need to be formally and explicitly reminded with some regularity that we are sinners. This sounds like a pretty bleak reason for taking part in a celebration, but the fact is that if we forget we are sinners, or if we choose to overlook the fact, we will soon find ourselves marooned, cut off from what gives meaning to our lives, striving to provide for ourselves that which only God and the Church can give us.

There is a kind of law of dissolution that is operative

in our lives, a natural tendency toward moral self-destruction. We naturally tend to think of ourselves first. We naturally tend to take the easy way out of situations, especially when the situations call for effort and sacrifice. We naturally tend toward a kind of false independence which leads us to believe that we can survive alone, stand on our own feet, make our own way. In our heart of hearts we know that this is not really the case, but our heart of hearts is often outshouted by other voices that seem more convincing.

Even when we are not dealing with matters of serious moral fault, we are still inclined to sin. We are inclined to little acts of selfishness. We are inclined to put off or diminish our contacts with the Lord in prayer. We are inclined to exclude God's call of love and generosity from various little corners of our lives. Left unattended, this law of dissolution can lead us, in the worst scenario, to a complete detachment from everything that is really significant for our lives. In a less catastrophic scenario, it can lead us to settle for superficiality and lukewarm indifference, instead of the life of energy and joy that God has planned for us.

This is why we need to look deep within ourselves once in a while and ask ourselves what we are all about. This is why we need to take stock of ourselves in the light of the two most important realities of our existence: the Lord and the Lord's Church. It is not healthy to live in a dream world, and a world of unacknowledged sinfulness is a dream world — which ultimately turns into a nightmare.

The second fundamental reason why we should participate regularly in the celebration of reconciliation is that we need to experience in our own individual lives the loving embrace of the Lord. It is all too easy for us to forget how important we are to God. We need the personal, radical reassurance that God loves us and cares for us in spite of our limitations and sins. We need to know that no matter where we have wandered, where we have failed, God still wants us.

We need to know that there is always someone to whom we can go, in whose sight we are still "all right." We need to celebrate, with the Church, the reality of God's immense and unfailing love for each one of us, a love that is not put off by our pettiness, a love that is greater than even our greatest sins, a love that stands with open arms to take us back from the most distant isolation.

In the Christian moral tradition, the only unforgivable sins are presumption and despair, either to think that we do not need God and God's love or to think that God cannot or will not continue to care for us. To a greater or lesser extent, these are the basic temptations of every Christian life. Every sinful act — great or small — is a step in one of these two directions. It is precisely to these two extremes of sin that the Sacrament of Reconciliation addresses itself by calling us to acknowledge our sinfulness and inviting us to celebrate the ever-present, all-embracing love of God.

## Frequency of Confession? Two Extremes to Be Avoided in Cases of Less Serious Involvement

If taking part in the celebration of reconciliation is important, even essential, for our well-being as individuals and as members of the Body of Christ which is the Church, we may ask ourselves how often and when we should use the sacrament.

If we are conscious of serious sin in our lives, we should come to the sacrament as soon as we can. There is no point in remaining in isolation when our heavenly Father stands waiting to welcome us home.

But what if our sins are not serious? What if we are conscious only of relatively minor transgressions that have not cut us off completely from God and the community life of the Church?

Here there are two extremes to be avoided. The first is to keep going to confession merely out of habit, confessing the same sins without any real intention of doing much about them, making the sacrament into a kind of spiritual mouthwash that we use regularly but could just as well do without.

The other extreme is not to go to confession at all. Our faith teaches us that there are other ways in which small sins can be forgiven: an act of contrition, an act of charity, the reception of Holy Communion. Why do we have to bother with confession? We may even find that the Sacrament of Reconciliation doesn't seem to do much for us, and that, no matter how hard we try, we keep falling into the same faults.

That may all be so, but the fact remains that sin and the forgiving love of God are such important realities in our lives that we need to give them explicit, detailed attention once in a while or we will begin to take them for granted. It is presumptuously easy to come to terms with our sins, big or small. It is desperately tempting to begin to think that God doesn't really care to bother with people like us.

Moreover, the difficulties we experience in eradicating our faults are signs of the deep roots that sin has in us. The Sacrament of Reconciliation is not some sort of magic that forces our free will into new paths in spite of itself. It is an encounter with God's love, to be sure. But even when our sins have been forgiven, the habits and inclinations that we have acquired for ourselves remain to be dealt with, again and again. The absence of obvious "results" from the Sacrament of Reconciliation is not an indication that nothing happens, but rather a reminder to us of the great part that sin plays in our lives and of the urgency of our need to be in touch with the enlivening love of our heavenly Father. Reconciliation is an act, but it is also a process.

**Recommended During Lent, Advent, Retreats, All Other Occasions for Spiritual Renewal**

The frequency of our use of the sacrament will depend on how serious we are about dealing with our sinfulness and how closely we wish to stay in touch with the forgiving, affirming, healing power of God. The Church calls on us in a particular way to give attention to repentance and renewal during the season of Lent.

Advent is another time in which the celebration of the Sacrament of Reconciliation receives special emphasis in the Church. Most believers find that a careful and serious use of the sacrament is very fruitful at times of retreat or during spiritual renewal programs. For that matter, the practice of monthly confession has a lot to be said for it. The important thing is that we be aware that the celebration of reconciliation is too crucial for our lives as Christians, either to make its use into mere routine or to neglect it.

Why take part in the celebration, then? Because it is a celebration in our honor. It is a celebration of our rescue from the desert isolation into which we had directed ourselves. It is a celebration that God hosts for us to welcome us back, to reassure us of our worth, to encourage us in our efforts to be faithful. It is a celebration that involves the whole Church, heavenly and earthly. It is a celebration that is too good to miss.